CHRONICLES OF FAITH

BEN-HUR

Lew Wallace

Retold by Dan Larsen

Illustrated by
Al Bohl

BARBOUR
PUBLISHING

Cover Illustration: Cory Godbey, Portland Studios, Inc.

Published by Barbour Publishing, Inc., P.O. Box 719, Uhrichsville, Ohio 44683, www.barbourbooks.com

Our mission is to publish and distribute inspirational products offering exceptional value and biblical encouragement to the masses.

 Member of the
Evangelical Christian
Publishers Association

Printed in the United States of America.

CHRONICLES OF FAITH

BEN-HUR

Rider and camel plodded toward the sun.

1

STAR SEARCHERS

Out of the Jebel es Zubleh Mountains and into the desert of Arabia came a traveler riding a camel. The traveler's face was burned brown by the sun, and the black beard that flowed over his face was streaked with gray. He wore a red kerchief on his head and a long white robe.

It was morning. Rider and camel plodded on toward the misty sun rising in the east. Two hours passed, then two more. There were no plants, no animals, no hills, only the wide sea of white sand and the hot sun now in a deep blue sky.

At midday the camel stopped. The rider dismounted, pulled a heavy pack from the camel's back, and set up a small tent. Inside he spread a carpet and laid out bread, dried

fruits, smoked mutton, and a leather bottle
of wine. He tied a bag of dried beans under
the camel's chin for the camel to eat as he
wished. Then the man stood and, shading
his eyes, scanned the horizon as if looking
for someone or something.

The afternoon passed. The man sat in
the tent, occasionally going outside to peer
off into the distance again. Finally he saw a
speck on the horizon. His eyes showed his joy
and eagerness at the sight. The speck grew
and grew. At last another camel with a rider
stopped just outside the first man's tent.

"Peace to you, O servant of the true
God," said the newcomer.

"And to you, O brother of the true faith,"
replied the first.

They embraced. The first traveler was
short and broad, the second tall and gaunt.
The first wore the robe and headdress of

The man scanned the horizon.

an Egyptian, the second the wide pants and short robe of a Hindu.

The Hindu's eyes now shone with tears. "God alone is great!" he said.

"And blessed are they that serve Him!" said the Egyptian. "But now see, the other comes!" He pointed north, where a third camel could now be seen coming toward them.

When the third man arrived, he dismounted and bowed to the two. "Peace to you, my brothers," he said. Unlike the Hindu and the Egyptian, this man's face was fair, his hair light and curly. He was bareheaded and wore a short tunic, his legs and arms bare, in the fashion of the Greeks.

"The Spirit brought me here first," said the Egyptian. "Thus I know I am chosen to be a servant to my brothers." He washed

The third man arrived.

the others' hands and feet in a bowl of water and dried them with a cloth. "Now come inside," he said. "I have food and drink."

After they had eaten, the Egyptian said, "Before us lie many days together. It is time we knew one another. So if it be agreed, let the one who came last be the first to speak."

So the Greek began. "My tale is a strange one," he said. "I do not understand any of this yet. All I know is that I am doing my Master's will. I know it is God's will because I am filled with joy serving Him.

"I am Gaspar of Athenia, in the land of Greece. My people have long thought that the mind is the best part of man. We are lovers of study and thinking. Our two greatest thinkers taught that every man has a soul and that there is only one God, who is always just. In my studies I

"I am a chosen servant."

strove to bring these ideas together, to find the relationship of God to a man's soul. There is no answer in our great schools. So one day I went to Mount Olympus in northern Thessaly. There I found a cave, where I stayed many days. I believed in God, and I believed He alone could give me the answer I sought, so I prayed day and night.

"My cave overlooked the sea. One day I saw a man flung overboard from a ship. He swam to my shore, and I called to him. I took care of him in my cave. He was a Jew. I learned from him that God does indeed exist and He had been the Jews' lawmaker, ruler, and King for ages. This Jew also said many of his people were expecting God to send a Savior to them in Jerusalem, their holy city. People are looking for this Savior even now, he said. 'Is this Savior only for the Jews?' I asked. 'No,' he said. 'God

"I saw a man flung overboard!"

has kept the Jews as His people so that through them the truth might be saved.'

"When the Jew had gone, I thought so much of these things. One night I sat in the doorway of my cave, looking at the sky. As I looked, I saw a star appear. It burned brighter and brighter and moved across the sky until it was right overhead. Then I heard a voice: 'Gaspar. Blessed are you! With two others from across the earth, you will see Him who is promised, and you will be witnesses for Him. In the morning rise, and the Spirit will guide you to meet these other two.' And with the Spirit guiding me, I traveled by ship and then by camel to this very spot here."

The Hindu and the Egyptian wept as they heard this story. Then the Hindu said, "I, too, have a strange tale to tell. My name is Melchior. I am a Hindu by birth. Our

"One night in the doorway of my cave. . ."

people believe in a supreme God, whom we call Brahm. Our sacred poems tell us of virtue, of good works, and of the soul. Our religion teaches that Brahm made four classes in all creation. First there are the spirits of heaven and earth. Then the Brahmans, those people most like God himself. Then the warriors, shepherds, farmers, and merchants. And last, the slaves and servants. My people believe that whoever is born in one of these classes cannot go higher or lower, but must remain as he is.

"I was born a Brahman. All my life, everything I did was directed by others. I was led, by sacred rituals and ceremonies and study, to follow the life of a Brahman. But I believed that God must be something more than that. I prayed to Him constantly. One day I discovered the truth that God

"I was born a Brahman."

is love. Thrilled with this, I preached it to everyone, but no one would listen. Some even tried to kill me, so strange was my idea that Brahm is love. The misery of my people made my love grow even more. So finally I went far up into the mountains, the Himalayas, where I could be alone with God. There I fasted and prayed for my people, asking God to show His love to them as He had to me. One night I saw a star, just as our friend the Greek did. I heard a voice saying the same things to me, and I have come here, led by the same Spirit."

"Your words, my brother," said the Egyptian, "are spoken in the Spirit of God, and it is in His Spirit that we understand them.

"My name is Balthasar," he continued. "My people of Egypt believed in one God,

"Some tried to kill me."

too—at first. But as the ages passed, we separated the one God into many, and then many more, and yet more. In this foolishness we lost our simple faith in a perfect God. But many years ago a people lived as slaves among my people. These were the Hebrews, who had their own religion and their own God. They were persecuted terribly. But one day their God delivered them in a way that my people have never forgotten. By this, their God was proved to be the true God. To this day, some of my people believe in the Hebrews' God. I am one of these.

"I, too, saw the star and heard the voice and am come, that we might see the Savior and worship Him. The voice said to me that we must go to the city of Jerusalem and ask where the King of the Jews is to be born."

"I, too, saw the star."

The three sat silently for some time, each lost in amazement. Then they rose, held hands, and prayed silently together. Without speaking, they packed up their things, climbed onto their camels, and set out.

The sun was sinking. The night was still, the air cool. The camels went in single file toward the west.

The sun dropped. The night grew cold. The moon rose. The camels went steadily on, casting long moon shadows across the sand.

Suddenly a dazzling light flared up ahead of the travelers, hanging in the sky just above the horizon. The men shouted together, "The star! The star! God is with us!"

In Jerusalem the people stared at the three travelers of the desert. The camels were unlike any the people had ever seen, so tall and majestic, and the riders were more wondrous still.

"The star! God is with us!"

The rich, embroidered trappings on the saddles and the large, colorful bundles strapped to the camels showed the riders to be rich men from distant lands—perhaps kings.

The three men asked everyone they met, "Where is He that is born King of the Jews?" But no one could answer. Some said, "Go to King Herod and ask him."

So they rode on, coming to the king's palace. When they asked Herod, the king's mouth dropped and his face grew ashen. *Another king!* he thought. Shaken, he called his priests, who knew what the prophets had written. They met and discussed the question for many hours. Later that night they went to the king. "It is written," said the chief priest, "that the Messiah is to be born in the city of David, Bethlehem of Judea."

Herod told this to the three travelers.

Another king! Herod thought.

Then he said, "Go and find this child and then come and tell me where He is, so I can come and worship Him, too."

The three then rode to Bethlehem, arriving on a clear night. As they entered the city, the star appeared again and traveled through the sky until it stopped directly over a small house on the outskirts of the city.

Here the three men found the child. His mother's name was Mary; her husband was Joseph, a carpenter from Nazareth. The three men knelt and worshipped the child. "How good is God!" said Balthasar, the Egyptian. "He has let us see the Savior." Then they gave the baby their gifts of gold, frankincense, and myrrh.

"This child is God's Chosen One," said Melchior, the Hindu. "He is sent to save men from their sins."

"This child is God's Chosen One!"

But that night an angel warned them not to return to Herod, so they returned to their homes by another way.

An angel warned them.

Messala and Judah

2

A Day of Changes

Twenty-one years after the birth of Christ, Valerius Gratus became the fourth imperial governor of Judea. He was unpopular with the Jews because he tightened Rome's grip on the whole province. His reign marked the beginning of the end of a long, bitter quarrel between the Romans and the Jews.

One day during this time, in a garden of the palace on Mount Zion, two youths sat talking. One was about nineteen, the other seventeen. Both were black haired and dark skinned. The elder, Messala, was a Roman; the younger, Judah, a Jew. The boys had been childhood friends. Messala's father was a Roman tax collector in Jerusalem. Messala had been sent to Rome to be educated, where he stayed for five years.

Now he was home again. He had gone a happy child and come back a Roman—vain, almost scornful, his lip curled slightly in a proud sneer as he spoke to his younger friend.

"A Jew never changes, does he?" said Messala, laughing. "Your lives go nowhere, just round and round. What is there in your religion but doddering old men arguing over worthless things? You have no poetry, no art. Your masters, your teachers—what are they, compared with our masters in Rome, who teach everything that is worth knowing?"

The Jew's face flushed. He had grown more and more sullen as the other spoke. Now he rose to leave.

"No, no, keep your place!" cried Messala.

"You mock me," said Judah.

"Hear me further," said Messala. "In my teacher's last lecture in Rome, he said,

Judah's face flushed in anger.

'Mars reigns, and Eros is dead.' He meant war is everything, love nothing. So it is with Rome. There is much in the world for us to conquer. See what possibilities lie before a Roman! I am a soldier. Why not you, too? I am a soldier now, but one day I will be a prefect. Think of life in Rome with money, wine, women, games, poets at the banquets, intrigues in the court, dice all the year round! You can share this with me. Judea is rich and ripe for plunder. When I have grown fat from her, I will make you high priest." He burst into laughter.

"We had better part," said Judah sadly. "I wish I had not come. I sought a friend and find a—"

"A Roman," said Messala, laughing again. "Be wise. Give up the follies of Moses and the traditions. They are dead things. Rome is the world now."

"Mars reigns, and Eros is dead."

Judah walked to the gate of the garden. "You have made me suffer today," he said. "You have convinced me that we can never be the friends we were, not ever." He left the garden.

Messala stood silently for a moment, as if thinking. Then he shrugged. "So be it," he said. "Eros is dead. Mars reigns."

Just off the Via Dolorosa, a main street in Jerusalem, sat the Hur house, enclosed by a thick stone wall. The house had two stories and was very well built and richly furnished. Judah's father had been a very rich merchant, but had been lost at sea many years earlier. The boy now lived here with his mother, younger sister, and their servants. Judah's favorite servant was Amrah, an old Egyptian woman who had served the Hurs for many years and was loved as one of the family.

"You have made me suffer today."

That afternoon when the boy came home, he flung himself onto a couch in the courtyard and lay with his face buried in his arms until evening.

Amrah came into the courtyard. "Supper is over, and it is late," she said. "Is my son not hungry?"

"No," he said.

"Are you sick?"

"No, not sick. Life does not seem so pleasant as it did this morning." But he would say nothing more.

Amrah loved the boy as her own son. "Your mother is on the roof," she said. "Go and talk to her."

The roof was like another room of the house. A low wall made of tiles ran around the edge.

There were chairs and couches for people to rest on and a little pavilion with

"Is my son not hungry?"

open sides in the center. Many houses in the region were like this. During the day people sought shelter from the desert heat, but at night the air was cool, the sky clear and beautiful. Upon the roofs, family members ate, slept, and gathered with friends.

Judah's mother was on the roof tonight. She lay on a couch in the pavilion, watching the stars. At her son's approach, she sat up. She could tell he was troubled.

"I visited Messala today," Judah said. "He is very much changed. He mocks our religion, our customs. He could have at least remembered our friendship. But he is no longer a friend. He is a—a Roman."

His mother was silent for a while, lost in thought. Finally she said, "There has never been a great nation that did not think itself superior to all others. When the Roman laughs at Israel, he repeats the

"I visited Messala today."

folly of other nations who have conquered us before. Egypt, Assyria, Macedonia—all have held Jerusalem, as Rome does now. But they have all gone, my son, and Jerusalem still stands, unchanged. He who laughs at Israel laughs at God."

Judah's eyes brightened a bit.

"There is no comparison possible between Israel and Rome," his mother continued. "While Israel has at times forgotten God, Rome never knew Him. We are God's people. He will answer any charges brought against us."

The boy's heart was beating fast. "And I?" he said. "What am I to be, Mother?"

"Just serve the Lord, the Lord God of Israel, not Rome," she said.

"May I be a soldier, then?"

"Yes. Did not Moses call God a man of war? But if you will be a soldier, serve

"He who laughs at Israel laughs at God."

the Lord, not Caesar." She rose then and, kissing her son good night, went inside.

Judah fell asleep on the roof. His heart no longer troubled him. When he woke, it was to the sound of music and singing. The sun was up, and his sister, Tirzah, sat near him. She was fifteen, as beautiful as her brother was handsome. She played a stringed instrument as she sang. Judah lay there smiling until she finished the song.

"Very pretty, my Tirzah, very pretty," he said.

She smiled. "The song?" she asked.

"Yes, and the singer, too. It sounds Greek. Where did you get it?"

"I heard it at the theater last month."

"Have you any more like it?"

"Yes, but not now. Amrah is bringing our breakfast to us up here. She says you are not well."

Tizrah played an instrument and sang.

"I'm fine," he said. And he told her of his visit with Messala the day before.

"What do you think, Tirzah?" he asked. "I am going away."

"Going away!" she said. "Where? When? For what?"

He laughed. "Three questions, all in one breath! I am going to Rome to be a soldier."

Her smile faded. "You will be killed!"

"If God wills, then yes. But, Tirzah, not all soldiers are killed."

She began to weep. "But we are so happy here. Stay with us. Why would you go off to Rome?"

"War is a trade. To learn it well, one must go to school, and there is no school like a Roman camp."

"But you would not fight for Rome?" she asked.

"I am going to Rome to be a soldier."

"Yes," he said, "if in return I learn how to fight against Rome one day. Now, be still! I hear Amrah coming. Say nothing of this to her."

The two had just started eating when suddenly the sound of trumpets rose from the street below. Brother and sister rushed to the wall to look.

Down the street came a procession of Roman soldiers. In the middle column of soldiers rode an official on horseback. He wore no armor and carried no weapon. His robe was embroidered with yellow silk. His appearance seemed to excite the anger of people along the street, who now could be seen learning over the walls of the roofs like the one on the Hur house. "Robber!" they shouted. "Dog of a Roman! Gratus the dog!"

Gratus! thought Judah. *So this is he. No*

A procession of Roman soldiers

wonder the people are so angry. All Jerusalem hated the Roman tyrant. But Judah's thoughts were not really on Gratus. He was watching the soldiers. *Look at the brawny limbs of those men! The sharp spears! The shiny helmets and breastplates!* In his excitement, he leaned farther over the wall.

Crack! A piece of tile broke loose under his weight. It began to fall, and the governor was directly below! Judah reached for the tile, shouting. Below on the street, faces turned up to see what looked like a boy throwing a heavy piece of tile down.

And as if the hand of fate stretched against the family of Hur, the tile struck the governor on the head and he fell from his horse as though dead.

Judah stumbled back from the wall, his face white. "Tirzah!" he cried. "I have killed the governor!"

Crack! A tile broke loose!

Now all along the street rose a cheer. The people saw the tile fall, saw the governor struck, and, like the soldiers, they thought the boy had thrown it. Now, goaded by the fall of their hated governor, the people swarmed into the street, attacking the soldiers with clubs, kitchen knives— anything they could grab. The battle surged all through the street, but it was a slaughter. The soldiers quickly cut their way through the mob.

The sound of cracking timbers and crunching stones came from below.

"They are taking our house!" Judah shouted.

Up came the screams and shouts of servants, the clang of swords and spears, and the tramp of soldiers' feet.

"Mother! Mother!" screamed Judah as he leaped down the stairs. Soldiers poured

The battle surged through the street!

into the courtyard through the broken-in gate.

"That is he!" came a sharp voice. Judah turned. Messala! He was pointing at Judah, his face twisted with hate.

"Him?" said a tall man in legionary armor. "He is but a boy!"

"Messala!" cried Judah. "My mother and sister! Help them! Remember our childhood, I pray you!"

Messala did not even look at Judah. He just turned on his heels and walked into the street.

Judah's heart turned to ice. Messala! "In the hour of your vengeance, Lord, let mine be the hand to deliver it to him!" he prayed.

In the street, the governor was being led off, his head wrapped. *So he is not dead!* thought Judah. *They will listen to me. They will understand it was an accident.*

"That is he!"

But his hands were tied behind his back. A trumpet sounded and the soldiers moved off down the street, pushing and dragging Judah along with them. He could not look back, could not see what had happened to his mother and sister. He pleaded with the tall soldier to let him explain to the governor.

The soldier's face was grim. "The governor has already determined your fate," he said. "Now move on and be silent!"

"It was an accident!"

The city of Misenum

3

BATTLE AT SEA

On the western coast of Italy, the city of Misenum sat atop a hill overlooking the bay of Neapolis. It was hard to tell which was bluer that day, the clear sky or the sparkling water of the bay. Softly, the waves rolled in to the white, sandy shore.

At anchor in the bay was half the reserve army of Rome, about a hundred warships. Their sails were furled, and in each ship a hundred and twenty long oars rested in the water, sixty to a side.

A stone wall surrounded the city on the hill. A narrow road passed through an opening in this wall and meandered down the hill to the bay. Along this road now came about thirty men, officials by their looks. They wore long white togas bordered with purple. The man leading was about fifty, slightly bald, and wearing a crown of laurel leaves.

When they reached the shore, the other men began to say their farewells to the one wearing the laurel crown.

"Where will you seek these pirates, my good Quintus Arrius?" asked one of the men.

"They were last seen in the Aegean Sea, according to the letter I received from Sejanus," said Arrius, a Roman tribune. "If you have any offerings, my friends, pray to the gods for good sailing and strong rowing. But look, there is my ship."

The ship was a fighter, long, narrow, and low. Just under the waterline on the front of the ship was a long, wooden beak, its tip shod with steel. This was used to ram enemy ships at sea.

A trumpet sounded on board and out

"There is my ship."

of the hatchways came the fighting men, lining up on deck. As one, they saluted the tribune. Sunlight gleamed off their polished helmets and shields.

"Now I am away to my duty, my friends," said the tribune.

"The gods go with you, O Quintus," said one of the men. They each came up to embrace the tribune.

"Farewell," he said. As he walked up the ramp to the ship, trumpets blared out from all the ships in the bay.

By noon the fleet was skimming the sea along the southwestern Italian coast. To a sailor or a merchant on shore, the sight of a hundred Roman warships could mean only one thing: Rome was looking for pirates! A group of about thirty Greek pirate ships had been ravaging the coasts in this area for many months. The reports

Rome was looking for pirates!

of these pirates, who plundered and sank ships, had reached Caesar, and now he was acting.

The tribune, Quintus Arrius, was an important military official in Rome. As commander of this fleet, he was under orders to attack and destroy the entire pirate fleet. He spoke to the chief of the rowers, a man called a hortator.

"My orders say we are to go past the Camponellan cape to Messina," said Arrius. "Beyond that, follow the bend of the Calabrain shore till Melito is on our left, then head eastward for Cythera. The gods willing, we will not anchor until we are in the Bay of Antemona. Our duty is urgent. We will need all speed. I am relying on you."

The hortator bowed and returned to his post. In the middle of the ship was a

Arrius spoke to the hortator.

cabin with the rowers' benches. In its front was a raised platform where the chief of the rowers sat beating on a basin to mark the tempo of the oars. Farther toward the front and above this platform was another platform, where the tribune sat. The rowers were slaves, all of them prisoners condemned to the galleys for life. They sat at their places and rowed, eating and sleeping during their brief rest periods. This was their whole life. A man condemned to the galleys usually lived no more than a year under such extreme circumstances. There were men of many sorts—blacks; Jews; Egyptians; Gauls; red-haired, blue-eyed giants of the Cimbri—each chosen for his brawn and endurance. Their names were forgotten; they were only known by the numbers painted at their places on the benches.

Marking the tempo

Arrius liked to watch the rowers. He was a lover of strength and physical sports. As he watched the men, he noted their various strengths or weaknesses, deciding who might need to be replaced by a fresh rower. He took particular interest in one, rower number Sixty. This one was no more than a boy. *Yet what a boy!* thought Arrius. His black hair was shaggy as a lion's mane and hung down to his shoulders. His beard was still scanty and barely covered his cheeks. His neck was thick, his shoulders rounded. Thick biceps rolled like melons under the strain of pulling on the oar. The sinews in his forearms stood out like steel cables. Under his grasp, his heavy oak oar almost bent to breaking.

By gods, what strength! thought Arrius. *He has spirit! I must know more of him.*

Two days later, Arrius told the chief to

Thought Arrius, *He has spirit!*

send Number Sixty to him on the deck.

The youth walked slowly up to Arrius, his face showing curiosity. In three years at the oars he had not once stepped outside the cabin.

"The hortator tells me you are his best rower," Arrius said.

"The hortator is very kind," said the youth.

"You have been here three years," said Arrius. "How is it that you have survived so long? Most men can only last a year here."

"The noble Arrius forgets that a man's spirit has much to do with his endurance. By its help, the weak sometimes thrive while the strong perish."

"By your speech, I know you are a Jew. I have not been to Jerusalem, but I knew of its Prince. He was fit to have been a King. What is your family name?"

"You have been here three years."

"My father was a prince of Jerusalem who was known and honored by the great Augustus of Rome. His name was Ithanar, of the house of Hur. I am Judah. By my father's family I would now be called Ben-Hur."

The tribune stepped back. "A son of Hur!" he said. "What has brought you here?"

"I was accused of trying to murder Valerius Gratus, the governor."

"You! You are that one?" The tribune's mouth was wide open. "I heard that story. I thought that family had been blotted off the earth."

There was pain in Ben-Hur's voice. "O noble tribune," he said, almost weeping, "my mother! And my little Tirzah! Can you tell me if they live? And if so, are they well?" His lips quivered. "That horrible day is three years gone now, but every hour has been an eternity to me. A lifetime in

"A son of Hur!"

a bottomless pit with death, and no relief but labor. And in all that time not a word from anyone, not a whisper. Oh, if in being forgotten we could only forget! If only I could hide from that scene—my sister torn from me, my mother's last look! I have felt the shock of ships in battle, felt the tempest lashing the sea, and laughed when others prayed. Death would be relief to me. In the strain of bending the oar, I have sought to escape the pain of that day. I can never be happy while they are lost. They call to me every night in my dreams." The tears poured down his cheeks. And now his voice turned bitter. "And mine was the hand that brought them down!"

"Do you admit your guilt then?" asked Arrius.

The youth's eyes flashed. "I swear by the God of my people, our God from the very

"My hands brought them down!"

beginning, that I am innocent!" he said.

The tribune's face grew troubled. "Did you not have a trial?" he asked.

"No."

"No trial!" cried the tribune. "No witnesses? Who judged you?"

"They bound me with cords," said Ben-Hur. "I saw no one. No one spoke to me. They dragged me to the seaside. I have been a galley slave since then."

Arrius was deeply troubled. The Romans were lovers of justice! It was impossible to condemn a man without a fair trial under Roman law. *What had happened here?* Arrius wondered. What horrible scheme—and whose—had it been to destroy this family? He believed Ben-Hur's story. The youth's feelings showed too strongly for his claim of innocence to be a lie. Arrius decided he would check into it when he returned to

What had happened here? Arrius wondered.

Rome. For now, he sent Ben-Hur back to his bench.

That night at his oar, Ben-Hur looked at the starry sky through his air vent. "O Lord," he prayed, "I am a true son of the Israel You have loved. Help me, I pray You!"

And all through the Roman fleet the message was stirring: The enemy has been sighted. Prepare for battle!

They came on the pirate fleet in the dark of night. The steel-shod prows of the Roman galleys battered the Greek vessels into splinters. Many sank immediately, but many more roused themselves for battle. From out of the darkness came battle cries, the clashing of spears as they cascaded onto the decks, and the splintering of wooden ships being smashed to pieces. And now fires flared up all over the ocean's surface as the Romans hurled burning oily rags

The clash of battle!

onto the enemy ships. Soon several ships were engulfed in roaring flames. Men dove screaming into the churning water.

The rowers could only hear the sounds of battle. They had been in many such battles, and their rowing did not change a beat. If their masters won this battle, nothing changed for the slaves. If the enemy won, the slaves might be taken by new masters, but their life of rowing would go on just the same. It made no difference to them.

During the battles at sea, the Romans chained the rowers' ankles so they could not escape. If a Roman ship was sunk, the slaves went down with it, chained to their benches. This was the one horror for a galley slave in battle, so they rowed fiercely, keeping their ship out of reach of enemy battering rams.

Ships were engulfed in flames!

But that night Arrius had told the chief to leave Ben-Hur's ankles free. *Why?* thought Ben-Hur. His heart was pounding. From up on deck came the clamor of shouting men and clanging swords and spears. The ship had been boarded by pirates! Ben-Hur dropped his oar. He sat still, the blood pounding in his temples. Suddenly he decided. He jumped from his bench, cleared the few stairs to the deck in one leap, and burst out of the cabin.

Just then the deck lurched. From below came a deafening *crunch*. Pirates had rammed the ship! Ben-Hur was thrown on his face. As he struggled to his feet, the sea rushed in through the wrecked side. A wall of water smashed into him and carried him overboard like a dry leaf in a tempest.

Ben-Hur struggled underwater until his lungs were ready to burst. When his head

Rammed!

shot up to the surface, the ship was gone. He swam to a floating timber and dragged himself onto it, clinging there, gasping for breath. Suddenly a Roman helmet emerged from the sea by his side, then a hand. Ben-Hur grabbed the wrist and heaved the man onto the timber. Arrius! His face was ghostly pale, his eyes wide and staring, but he was still alive. His breath came in shallow gasps, his lips trembling.

Through the night Ben-Hur lay on the timber as the battled continued. The timber drifted farther and farther away. When morning came, Arrius woke. He stared around him at the calm sea and at Ben-Hur.

Then he struggled to sit up, reaching a hand to Ben-Hur. "Son of Hur," he said, "I knew your father and loved him. You have

Ben-Hur heaved the man onto the timber.

saved me. If we are rescued, I swear to you that I will take you to Rome. You will be my son and heir. Everything I have will be yours!"

"Everything I have will be yours!"

Ben-Hur, adopted son of Arrius

4

SON OF ROME, SON OF ISRAEL

Up the river Orantes to the docks of Antioch in Assyria came a transport galley. It docked and began to unload cargo on the busy wharf as several passengers stepped ashore. One of these walked up the narrow street into the city. His white robe flowed over him loosely, yet it was stretched taut over his broad shoulders. The hands and forearms that hung from his short sleeves showed an immense strength. Three years as a galley rower and five more in the best military schools of Rome had developed Ben-Hur to the peak of his physical powers. Five years as the adopted son of the Roman tribune Quintus Arrius had also developed a noble manner. Ben-Hur's movements were smooth and graceful, barely concealing his explosive strength.

Arrius the tribune had died at sea three years ago, leaving Ben-Hur sole heir to his vast estate in the city of Misenum. The young Hur, now calling himself Arrius, had been trained in the military schools, learning all the arts of weapons and fighting. He had been an eager pupil, his hatred for Rome and his desire for revenge driving him on. He attacked his training with a ferocity that eventually earned him a reputation throughout Rome. For his swordsmanship and his wrestling skills, he had become famous in the palestra, the training school of the gladiators.

At Arrius' death, Ben-Hur took over his father's duties. He was in Antioch now on official business. But just now he had another purpose. He walked quickly through the winding street that bustled

On official business

with merchants and peddlers with laden carts. He turned onto a street that led past the wharves by the shore. It went through an old stone gateway and under the Selucian bridge, a great arched walkway overhead. Here Ben-Hur stopped. Under the bridge was a gray stone house with a heavy wooden door. He knocked and a porter answered.

"I wish to see Simonides the merchant," said Ben-Hur.

"This way, sir," said the porter. He led Ben-Hur by a path through stacks and stacks of boxes and bags of cargo, up a stairway, to a small stone building on the roof. "There," said the porter.

Ben-Hur called at the door.

"In God's name, come in," said a little man. He was sitting, or seemed to be propped up, on a heap of cushions on the floor. His

"This way, sir."

head rested on his chest as if he had no neck. His body was a shapeless lump under a loose silk robe. By his side stood a girl, black-haired and beautiful. She looked at Ben-Hur.

"Are you Simonides, merchant and Jew?" asked Ben-Hur.

"I am he," said the man. "And this is my daughter, Esther. Please state your business, sir."

"I am the son of Ithanar, late head of the house of Hur in Jerusalem," said Ben-Hur.

The merchant's right hand closed tightly into a fist for an instant.

"I heard a tale on my voyage to Antioch," continued Ben-Hur. "A certain man on board told me of a man named Simonides who has become very wealthy by trading. This man said that Simonides had been chief servant of my father in Jerusalem and managed my

"I am Simonides."

father's business from Antioch."

The merchant's face seemed pale, and his hand again closed tightly, but he said nothing.

"I also heard that this Simonides was sought by the governor Gratus and tortured until he confessed that his wealth was illegal," said Ben-Hur.

"You have heard rightly in one thing," said Simonides. "I was indeed tortured, twice. My body was broken. It is now useless to me. But Gratus could not break my spirit. My wealth is from trading and is legally mine. As to the other, yes, I knew your father, but that is all I will say. First, I must see proof that you are who you say you are."

Proof! Ben-Hur had not thought of that. "I can prove my Roman identity," he said, "but not my other." He told Simonides

Searching for information

his story, from the accident to Gratus to the present. "But do not think that I have come to demand my father's property," continued Ben-Hur. "You may keep all of it. All I wish to know is whether my mother and sister still live, and where. Can you tell me?"

"I have heard of the tragedy to your family," said Simonides. "And I did seek to know whether your mother and sister are alive. But no one has heard of them since that day. I believe they are lost."

Ben-Hur struggled against tears. "Then I, too, am lost!" he said. He turned to leave. "I pray for your pardon for my intrusion." His voice shook slightly. "I would not have troubled you at all but for my sorrow. Now I have nothing to live for but revenge. Farewell."

"Peace go with you," said Simonides.

Ben-Hur struggled against tears.

Esther could not speak. She was sobbing, her face in her hands.

As soon as Ben-Hur was gone, Simonides turned to his daughter. A smile lit his pallid face. "Esther, quick!" he said. "Bring Malluch to me."

Ben-Hur wandered about the city aimlessly. On hearing about Simonides a hope had sprung up in his heart, but now it was crushed again. One thought would sustain him: *Vengeance! Rome will pay!*

Now as he walked, great crowds of people began pushing past him. They were moving quickly. He went with them to see where they were going. Soon a man appeared at his side, wearing a simple robe and carrying a wooden staff. On his head was a brown cloth tied with yellow rope.

"Sir," said Ben-Hur, "are you a Hebrew? You have the look of one."

A stranger at his side

"That I am," said the man, smiling. "I am from Jerusalem. Are you going my way?"

"I will gladly. Where are all these people going?"

"To the stadium. The chariots are practicing today. Come."

The two men talked as they went. In response to the stranger's questions, Ben-Hur would only tell him that he was a Jew but an official of Rome, in Antioch on business. But Ben-Hur began to like this man. It had been so long since he had seen a countryman. He asked the stranger for any news he had from Jerusalem.

The stadium was filling with people. Ben-Hur and the Jew took seats near the arena. The chariots were circling the track slowly, parading all their finery. One particular chariot caught Ben-Hur's eye. It was Roman in style and lavished with gold

The chariots circled slowly.

trappings. As it came around the bend, he could see the driver's face.

Messala!

Ben-Hur's heart jumped. There was that slight sneer, that proud tilt of the head. How long had he waited for a chance to meet him again? And how long had he nursed thoughts of revenge? Now here he was!

Just then his attention was drawn by a man's shouting. In front near the track stood a bearded man in a turban, waving his arms to the spectators. "Men of the East and West, hearken!" he cried. "I bring you word from Sheik Ilderim. With four horses he comes up against the best here. He needs a mighty man to handle them. To whomever can handle them in the chariot race, he promises riches forever! I say to you all, tell everyone of his offer."

"Who is this man he speaks of?" Ben-Hur

"The sheik needs a mighty man!"

asked his companion.

"Sheik Ilderim is a mighty man of the desert," said the Jew. "He has many people, many horses, many camels. Some say he controls all the goings to and fro in the desert."

Ben-Hur could barely control his excitement. "My friend," he said, "tell me. Can a man forget his mother?"

"If he is an Israelite, never!" said the other. "Our commandment is, 'Honor your mother and father as long as you live.'"

"By your words I know you are a true Jew," Ben-Hur said. "And I know that I can trust you. Listen. I know that man there." He pointed to Messala. Then he told the Jew as much of the story as he dared, leaving out his real name and his life as a slave on the galley.

"Tell me," continued Ben-Hur. "Do you

Ben-Hur could barely control his excitement!

know where to find this Sheik Ilderim? I wish to be his driver."

"Do you know how to drive?" asked the Jew.

"I was trained by the best in Rome. I have driven chariots for the emperor himself."

"The sheik is camped in the Orchard of Palms. I can take you to him."

"Can we go tonight?"

"We can start right now."

"You are a true friend! But tell me, what is your name?"

"I am Malluch," said the man, bowing.

It was two hours by horse to the Orchard of Palms, but Ben-Hur and Malluch talked as they rode.

"For his treachery and his taking my mother and sister from me, I wish to punish this man Messala," said Ben-Hur. "Will you help me?"

To the Orchard of Palms

"I am a Jew, not a Roman," said Malluch. "As you are a Jew, we are brothers. Yes, I will help you. I am no friend of Rome. And it is the Law of Moses: An eye for an eye and a tooth for a tooth."

"Is this chariot race an important event here?"

"In Antioch there is none more important. Thousands upon thousands of people from all over the world will be here."

For the first time in many years, Ben-Hur smiled.

Ben-Hur smiled.

The four horses handled as one.

5

A RACE FOR REVENGE

The four horses were Arabians—beautiful, graceful, strong. Under Ben-Hur's hand they drove as one horse, flowing swiftly across the sand. Sheik Ilderim and Malluch stood watching as Ben-Hur practiced. The sheik's eyes were dancing.

"It takes a gifted hand to make those horses run like that," he said. "But, see? They are yet just loping. When they are given rein, none can match them!"

Ben-Hur and Malluch had arrived last night. The sheik greeted Malluch as an old friend. Ben-Hur wondered about this. Then he offered to drive the sheik's horses. He suggested that he would try them today. Ilderim could watch them before deciding on him as a driver. The sheik agreed. He then served them richly. They ate and drank sitting on thick cushions in the sheik's tent.

For hours the next day, Ben-Hur drove the horses. Then he ate with the sheik again that night.

"I have a guest with me," said the sheik. "He is dining with us tonight. He has a story to tell that an Israelite should never tire of hearing. Ah, here he is. Come in, Balthasar, my friend."

An old man entered the tent. His beard was even longer and whiter than the old sheik's. He wore a black robe. "To you and your friend I give peace and the blessing of the one true God," he said.

As they ate, Balthasar the Egyptian told Ben-Hur the story of the meeting of the wise men and the birth of the Messiah. As Ben-Hur listened, the beating of his heart quickened.

Balthasar the Egyptian

"And when we had seen the child in Bethlehem," Balthasar said, "we were warned in a vision not to tell Herod, the king, because he would try and kill the child. And the husband of the child's mother was warned to take the child and flee into Egypt."

Ben-Hur believed every word of this. He was a Jew and was taught the laws and promises of the holy scriptures. He well knew the promise of the coming King of the Jews. "So," he said, "this King must be alive now."

"He would be about your age," said Balthasar.

"And this King is to rule all of Israel?"

"His kingdom will last forever."

A new thought struck Ben-Hur. A King! A King to rule all Israel, to destroy Roman power forever! He stayed awake

"He would be about your age."

long into the night, thinking, too excited to sleep.

The next morning a messenger rode up to the camp. "The merchant Simonides wishes to see you," he said to Ben-Hur.

When he stepped inside the roof office of Simonides later that day, Ben-Hur stopped short and blinked in surprise. There sat the merchant and his daughter as before, but with him now were the sheik, Balthasar, and the Jew named Malluch.

"What does this mean?" asked Ben-Hur. There was danger in his voice.

"Please sit down," said Simonides, pointing to a chair.

As Ben-Hur listened in amazement, the merchant told him he had sent his servant, Malluch, to watch him, to see whether he was really who he claimed to be. Malluch reported that Ben-Hur did indeed seem to

Too excited for sleep

be telling the truth.

Simonides pointed to the sheik and Balthasar. "These, too, are my friends," he said. "They, too, have talked with you, and they speak well of you. I am indeed your father's servant. During his life I operated here in Antioch. When that Roman dog took your mother and sister and your home, he had me brought to him to get from me the rest of your father's wealth. I refused him, so he had me tortured, twice. The second time, when they brought me home, broken as you see me now, my beloved wife, Rachel, fell dead of grief at seeing me." His eyes filled with tears. His daughter clutched his shoulder.

"But Gratus could not take from me what I was entrusted by your father to keep," continued Simonides. "Now I return to you all I have earned. The total of your

His eyes filled with tears.

wealth, son of Hur, is 673 talents, making you the richest subject in the world!"

Ben-Hur stammered, "Dear Simonides— my father's faithful servant! How could a man be better served? I wish to free you from your servitude. All that you have, all you have earned, I give you and your daughter. It is all yours to keep."

"No, good master," said Simonides, "I chose to be your father's bond servant for life because I loved him. I do not wish the service to end with his son. Let me remain as your servant. Only entrust the managing of your property to me, as your father did. This is all I ask of you."

"As you wish," said Ben-Hur, bowing.

"There is one more thing I would ask of you," said Simonides.

"It is yours."

"Balthasar has told you of the coming

"You are the richest subject in the world!"

King. This King is no doubt somewhere preparing for the moment He declares Himself. When He comes He will need the power to crush Rome. With your wealth and your mastery of the arts of war, you could be of more service to Him than anyone on earth."

Ben-Hur's hands gripped the arms of his chair. His heart was pounding.

"Think of my grievance with Rome!" continued Simonides. "Is it not at least equal to yours? With our wealth we could arm thousands of faithful Israelites to fight for the King. And you yourself could train them and lead them in battle. The good sheik will help you. He will show you the most desolate places in the desert, where the troops can train. His people control the desert. They will guard you."

"And when the King makes His

His heart pounded.

appearance, His army will be ready and waiting!" cried Ben-Hur.

Simonides nodded. "And what better revenge against Rome could you and I wish for?" he said.

The old Egyptian shook his head sadly. "Ah, you do not understand," he said. "The King will not come with swords. The kingdom He rules does not belong to this earth. He has come to save men's souls, not to save Israel from Rome."

Ben-Hur seemed not to hear. "I will begin as soon as possible," he said, rising. "I will work from the desert, and you, my good Simonides, from your seat in Antioch here. But first I have a score to settle with an old enemy. I must get the horses ready!"

Back at the sheik's camp, Ben-Hur drove the horses for several hours daily. He was

"I must get the horses ready!"

an expert in chariot racing, and he knew these were the best horses he had ever driven. All through Antioch, excitement was mounting over the day of the race. Huge bets had been placed, most of them on Messala, and Messala had bet his entire fortune on himself. This was even better than Ben-Hur had hoped for. If Messala lost, he would not only be shamed in all of Rome, but he would be brought to poverty as well. The taste of revenge grew sweeter in Ben-Hur's mouth with each passing hour.

One afternoon Sheik Ilderim came to Ben-Hur. He was holding a letter. His face was grave. "My people guard all roads through the desert," he said. "Early this morning one of my men stopped a courier on his way to Jerusalem. This courier carried a letter from Messala to Governor Gratus."

These were the best horses he'd ever driven.

Ben-Hur's face suddenly paled.

"Messala told the governor that the man they had sent away to be a galley slave was in Antioch. He also said that if this man, Ben-Hur, were not destroyed, then all the wealth he, Messala, and the governor had stolen from the family of Hur might be lost to them."

Ben-Hur could not speak. His heart was racing. He turned, stumbled into his tent, and lay panting on the ground. How? How could Messala have known? Had he recognized him? Had someone told him? It *must* have been a plot all along: Messala and Gratus had used the accident to Gratus as an excuse to put Ben-Hur and his mother and sister away, to steal their property.

The sheik entered Ben-Hur's tent. "After the race we must flee," the sheik

Shocking news!

said. "Gratus will send troops here to destroy us. Messala knows about me. He knows you are staying with me. We are not in danger until after the race, but then we must flee and leave no trace. They cannot pursue us into the desert. The desert is mine. They know that there my people would hunt them down and destroy them like wandering cattle. I will stand by you, Ben-Hur. And I will help you prepare your army in the desert for the coming King."

Ben-Hur stood and embraced the sheik. "Tomorrow," he said. "Tomorrow I will have my revenge against Messala. And his destruction will be our first strike against Rome."

At three o'clock the next afternoon, the stadium was filled with people. They had come from as far away as Rome to see this chariot race. They chanted and waved banners for their favorites.

"Tomorrow I will have my revenge!"

Just then the trumpets sounded. Out came the chariots. The crowd roared. The chariots slowly circled the track, each carrying a flag of a different color: Ben-Hur's was white, Messala's was scarlet. These were the colors waved by most in the crowd. Of the two, there were perhaps more white than red.

Eight chariots circled the dusty track. A hundred thousand spectators shouted and waved and pounded their feet on the stone steps of the vast Olympic stadium. In the front row were the sheik, Balthasar, Simonides, Malluch, and Esther. She alone in all that crowd was silent. She watched Ben-Hur.

The chariots came around the bend once more and drew together in a line across the track. Then a trumpet sounded, and the race was on.

Messala was in front. In the stadium

Chariot race

his color waved wildly. Thirty-two horses pounded around the track, whips lashing over their backs, dirt clods flying.

Two laps were down, Messala still led. The sneer on his face seemed to widen with each trip around the track. Ben-Hur's face was calm, but his jaw was set firmly. He seemed strangely reserved, as if waiting for something.

Four laps were down. Ben-Hur had pulled even with Messala. Suddenly Messala lashed out with his whip, striking Ben-Hur across the cheek. Ben-Hur staggered and almost fell. A gasp went up from the crowd. The Romans among the crowd cheered and shouted Messala's name.

But Ben-Hur recovered, though he had lost ground. Five laps. Six. Messala had stretched his lead. A cold light shone in

Messala lashed Ben-Hur with his whip!

his eyes. His teeth were set in a hard grin. Now Ben-Hur was only mid-pack.

Seven laps. "Messala! Messala!" came the chants. Only Ben-Hur's small group of friends sat unmoving, unspeaking. The sheik's face was pale, his lips tight. Esther was weeping.

Eight laps. Nine. The sheik dropped his chin to his chest. He seemed shrunken. His lips quivered.

Ten laps. "Look!" cried Esther.

Messala was way out in front, but now Ben-Hur's chariot broke from the pack, his whip snaked over the Arabian's backs as they leaped forward. Around the turn came Messala and Ben-Hur, almost together. Suddenly Ben-Hur jerked his reins, bringing his chariot wheel just inside Messala's. His wheel touched the other's axle. *Crack!* Messala's chariot lurched,

Ben-Hur jerked his reins!

throwing him over the front. He tumbled along the track under the wheels of the chariot, then lay still in the dust, and Ben-Hur drove across the finish line the victor.

Messala was thrown!

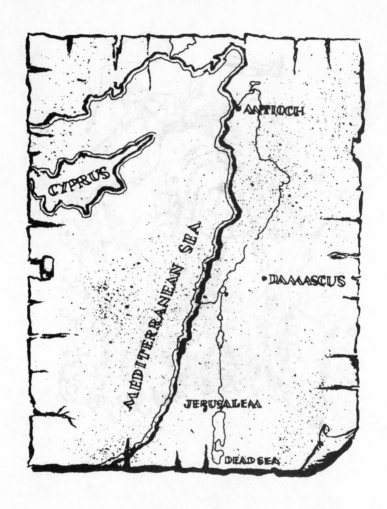

From Antioch to Jerusalem

6

Home to Jerusalem

The first thing Simonides did with Ben-Hur's money was rid Jerusalem of Valerius Gratus, governor of Judea. Simonides paid Sejanus, the imperial favorite in Rome, five talents in Roman money to remove Gratus from office. In Gratus's place, Sejanus appointed Pontius Pilate.

Simonides did this for Ben-Hur, who was going to Jerusalem to look for his mother and sister. Without Gratus, Ben-Hur would be freer to search the city.

While Gratus had been cold and hateful, Pilate had some measure of good in his heart. The first thing he did in office was review the records of all prisoners Gratus had kept. Many of these prisoners were set free from the vast dungeons under the palace tower.

One particular cell was discovered deep underground. Gratus had erased all records of this cell from the prison documents. It was sealed off from all the others. He had told the warden that two men with leprosy, both condemned to life in prison for murder, were kept there. No one but Gratus knew who the occupants were.

When the cell was opened, there were not two men but two women inside. They were naked and starved almost to death. Their thin white hair hung in tatters. And worse—they were lepers! Their lips and noses had been half eaten by the disease. Their skin was sickly white and covered with scaly patches; their voices were shrill and harsh. Seeing them, the warden drew back in horror.

They were given clothes and set free. That night the two women hobbled

The warden drew back in horror.

through the dark city streets, holding on to each other for support. They stared about them in wonder, as if seeing the outside world for the first time.

Slowly, painfully, they made their way through the city. Halfway down the street named Via Dolorosa, they stopped at a large house enclosed by a stone wall. The house was dark. Vines and creepers covered the stone wall. The gates had been sealed with mortar and timbers. A plaque on one gate read, THIS IS THE PROPERTY OF THE EMPEROR.

The women stood for a long time, looking at the house and weeping. Suddenly one grabbed the other's arm "Mother!" she whispered. "There is someone lying under the tree by the gate."

Just then the figure turned, and the moon shone on his face.

Painfully walking down the Via Dolorosa

"Judah!" gasped one of the women. "It is my Judah!" The other woman started across the street, but was grabbed by the first. "No, Tirzah!" she whispered sharply. "Do not touch him! We are lepers. If you touch him, he will get the disease."

They stood there, wringing their hands and weeping bitterly. Then one of them crept across the street to the sleeping man. She knelt at his feet. "Judah, my son, my dear son," she sobbed softly. "I shall never see you again. But it is enough that God has let me see that you live, and that you are well." And she kissed the dirty soles of his sandals. Then she went back to the other woman. They continued on down the street, looking back at the man, their weeping growing louder and more agonized as they went.

Soon they came to a gate in the city

"I shall never see you again."

wall, turned, and went out into the desert.

They did not see the silent figure stealing down the street and stopping at the house they had just left. The figure almost stumbled over the sleeping man.

"Judah!" came a woman's voice. The man woke. He stared up at the little woman wrapped in a cloak and shawl.

"Amrah!" he cried. "Is it you?" He climbed to his feet.

"It is," she said. "And praise to the God of your race! I thought you were long dead."

They held each other tightly, sobbing and laughing.

"It is a long time since I heard my boyhood name, Judah," said the man. "I have taken my father's name now—Ben-Hur."

"Come inside," said Amrah. She reached a hand through the timbers in the gate. There was a *click*, and the gate swung open.

"Amrah! Is it you?"

They went quickly across the dark, silent courtyard. Tall weeds grew in cracks among the flagstones. The walls of the house were darkened with disuse, and here and there were patches of lichen.

Inside, Amrah drew a shutter across a window and lit a small lamp. And there in the dim light stood Amrah as Ben-Hur remembered her. Amrah, the beloved, faithful maidservant. She was a bit older looking, a bit more stooped, but her loving gaze was just the same.

"Amrah," said Ben-Hur, "how is it that you are here? Have you lived here alone all this time?"

She nodded. Her eyes glistened. "Perhaps you did not see," she said, "but that evil day the soldiers came into our home and took— took—" She began sobbing, her face in her hands. "When they took your dear little

There stood Amrah.

sister Tirzah, your mother, and you, the soldiers grabbed me, too. But I broke away and fled through the confusion back into the house. I was sealed in. I had food enough for a while, but soon I needed to go into the city. I worked away at the mortar on the gate we entered tonight until I had loosened enough so I could work the latch. From the outside it still appears sealed. I go out and buy food only at night, and I have lived here in secret all these years. I have prayed every day that someday at least one of you would return to me. And now you have come, my Judah."

She held out her arms to him and wept on his shoulder as they held each other.

"You must tell me, Amrah," he said, "though my heart fails me as I ask. Are my— Have you heard anything about my mother and sister?"

There was pain and bitterness in her

Amrah wept in his arms.

voice as she said, "They were taken to the dungeons under the tower and have not been heard of since. I fear— I have been afraid for years that they are dead."

"Oh, Amrah," sobbed Ben-Hur. "This is a bitter homecoming."

"I fear they are dead!"

"Our waiting is at an end!"

7

PREPARING FOR THE KING

Across the desert came a lone rider on a horse. He climbed several low hills, then descended onto a large, circular plain neatly hidden from view.

The rider stopped before a cave in a hillside and from out of the cave came a black-bearded man wearing a Roman breastplate over a Jewish tunic. The rider handed him a letter.

As he read it, his cheeks flushed and a wide grin spread across his face. "My friends!" he called. "Our waiting is at an end!"

Several dark-haired, swarthy men, also dressed as the speaker, came out of the cave. "What does the letter say, Commander?" asked one of the men.

"It is from my friend Malluch in

Antioch," said the first. "He says that a man called John has been proclaiming a coming King and that the King will come to Jerusalem very soon."

At this a great cheer rose up from the men. Now the man with the letter said to the messenger. "Wait for me one moment. I will be with you again shortly." He quickly disappeared into the cave. A few minutes later he came out with two letters and gave them to the messenger.

"Take these with great haste," he said. "One is to my servant Simonides in Antioch, the other to Sheik Ilderim."

The messenger bowed and then returned the way he had come.

Then the speaker said to two of his men, "Saddle my horse and get provisions ready for me. Tonight I ride to Jerusalem!"

"Take these with great haste."

The night was cold, clear, and dark. There was no moon to light the path of a traveler, only the star-speckled sky. Just the sort of night for a traveler wishing to go unseen.

Tonight the traveler was Ben-Hur. He spurred his horse southward across the wide desert. There was no road here. Few travelers except the desert jackal ever went this far north. Here an army could camp for years undiscovered.

An army did camp here. The camp lay in the hidden valley Ben-Hur had left just hours earlier. He had gathered ten thousand men from Galilee to prepare his army for the coming King. All through the winter months he had trained the troops in the desert. He drilled them in the Roman legion's method of combat. Simonides bought the weapons and armor and horses;

The night was cold, clear, and dark.

Sheik Ilderim and his people made sure no one discovered Ben-Hur's training camp.

The Galileans had proved eager for the task. Their hatred for the Romans was even greater than their love for their own country. Of all the peoples of Israel they were the most fiercely independent, the most ready to revolt against Rome. As Ben-Hur went through their region, telling of the coming King, more and more Galileans joined him.

And they learned quickly. At the end of that spring, Ben-Hur felt his troops were ready.

And now this letter from Malluch! The King's arrival in Jerusalem could mean one thing: He was ready to proclaim Himself. When He did, Ben-Hur would be there, ten thousand troops at his call.

They could easily crush any opposition

The Galileans learned quickly.

in Jerusalem. Their success would bring many more thousands of Israelites to the new King's side. At last Rome would meet an enemy more than its match!

Ben-Hur was still on the desert when dawn came. He stopped to rest his horse. In the growing light he saw a camel in the distance, coming toward him. On the camel's back was a square tent of cloth.

The camel stopped before Ben-Hur. The tent flap was drawn aside, and there sat the old Egyptian, Balthasar.

"I give you God's greetings, son of Hur," said the Egyptian.

"The peace of the Lord to you," said Ben-Hur, bowing. "I am soon coming to a small stream where there are trees and soft grass. Please join me."

"I thank you. Lead on and I will follow."

A camel approached.

In about two hours they came to the stream, where they rested on the grass. Ben-Hur wanted to hear more about the Messiah, the coming King. He showed Balthasar the letter from Malluch.

Balthasar's face seemed to brighten as he read it. Then he closed his eyes and lifted his hands. "You have been very good to me, O God," he said. "Let me, I pray, see Your Savior just once more, that I might worship Him again before I die."

Suddenly Ben-Hur remembered, or thought he remembered, something Balthasar had said in the office of Simonides a year ago: *He has come to save men's souls, not to save Israel from Rome.*

Ben-Hur frowned as he thought of this. "O noble Egyptian," he said, "do you still believe the Messiah's kingdom is not of this earth?"

"Is the kingdom not of this earth?"

"I do," said Balthasar.

"Let us go to Jerusalem together, where we will see Him."

"Ah yes, you have been preparing." The Egyptian's face was stern, but his eyes were soft. "You are going to see a king of men. I am going to meet a Savior of souls. I have much hope for the salvation of my soul. God has given us a good life here on earth. But there is a new beginning at death, a new life. As well as He has provided for us in this life, He has provided much more for the next. His Anointed One has come to offer life to anyone who believes in Him. Man has need of a savior so much more than a king. What is an earthly ruler—a warrior—compared to a King whose kingdom lasts forever?"

Ben-Hur could say nothing. They packed up in silence and rode on.

"I'm going to meet a Savior."

Three days later they came to Bethabara by the Jordan River. Colored booths and tents were set up all along the shore. People were everywhere. *What is going on?* wondered Ben-Hur. *A festival?*

A man in a course, brown tunic and long, shaggy hair was speaking to a group of people by the shore. Ben-Hur stopped a man going by. "Who is that man by the shore?" he asked.

"He is called John," said the man. "John the Baptist."

Suddenly the man called John pointed up the river, where another Man was walking toward them. He wore a white robe that was well worn and travel stained. His hair and beard were the color of chestnut. His figure was rugged, His hands thick and sinewy, but His manner was calm, peaceful. He walked slowly.

John the Baptist

Balthasar was staring at the Man as if in a trance. Ben-Hur's heart leaped. Why? What was there about this Man? His eyes! They were as clear as desert pools and seemed to hold all the light of the sun.

Then came John's voice. "Behold the Lamb of God, who takes away the sin of the world!"

"Behold the Lamb!"

"The coming King is on His way!"

8

A Healing Reunion

A courier rode up to the house of Hur on the Via Dolorosa in Jerusalem. He gave a letter to the servant at the gate. "To the master of the house, Simonides, from the son of Hur." The servant went quickly to the roof of the house, where Simonides and his daughter sat.

"Tell me," said Esther excitedly, as her father read the letter. "What does it say?"

"It says that the coming King is on His way now to Jerusalem!" said Sominides, his hand shaking. "And Ben-Hur has sent two legions of troops following. He himself will come here tonight. He says the King announced that He was going to Jerusalem, where everything the prophets had written would now come true."

The Hur house was filled with life once more. Simonides had bought it from Pontius Pilate and restored it to its original splendor. Simonides, his daughter, and the old Egyptian, Balthasar, had come to live there. And Amrah, to her delight and pride, was once again the chief maidservant.

It was the twenty-first day of March, three years after the Messiah had come to John at Bethabara. Ben-Hur had stayed in the desert, gathering and training troops and following the news of the coming King of Israel. For three years now the King had been going all over Judea, proclaiming the kingdom of God. Everywhere there was great talk of the many miracles this King was doing. He made the blind to see, the lame to walk. He even raised the dead to life.

Ben-Hur had been very troubled when he had gone to Jerusalem to see this King

Ben-Hur training his troops

three years ago. He had thought the King was going to take His throne then, but nothing happened. Ben-Hur returned to the desert angry and confused. *What is the King waiting for?*

As time went by, Ben-Hur wondered more and more whether Balthasar was right. Was the coming King not of this world?

It had been a lonely, frustrating time of waiting for Ben-Hur. He had lost all hope that his mother and sister were alive. He would remain a fugitive as long as Gratus still lived in Rome. He was denied a peaceful life like other men, with a wife, a family, a home. His life was in the desert, training for war. And more and more, the pretty face of Esther, the merchant's daughter, came to him in his dreams at night.

He came tonight to his father's house. He climbed the stairs to the roof, where the

Esther filled his dreams at night.

merchant and his daughter sat with Balthasar. He bowed to the three and they exchanged greetings. Ben-Hur's gaze rested the longest on Esther, then he quickly turned away. He had not meant to stare at her! *How beautiful she has become!* he thought.

"I bring news of the King," he said, taking a seat. There was eagerness in his voice.

Just then Amrah appeared. "Dear Amrah," said Ben-Hur. "Have you—have you heard anything of them?"

She shook her head quickly. Her hands played nervously with her shawl. She retreated into a shadow and sat down.

Ben-Hur was silent for a moment. He took steady, deep breaths, as if to control a sob.

"Tell us of the King," said Balthasar.

Ben-Hur looked at the old Egyptian. "Maybe you are right," he said. "Maybe this Man is a savior, not a king."

How beautiful she has become! he thought.

He looked at Simonides. "He does not look like a king," said Ben-Hur. "And He does not travel like a king. Many, many days I have been among the crowds that follow Him. He travels with twelve men whom He calls His disciples. They are not royalty, but fishermen, tax collectors, tillers of the soil. They own nothing, take nothing with them. They travel on foot in the desert and sleep in the open with no tent.

"And yet," he continued, "His power is greater than any man's on earth, greater than any king's! I have seen Him heal the sick with just a spoken word. I have seen Him make the dumb to speak, the lame to walk, the blind to see. At the gates of Nain He said to a dead boy, 'Get up,' and the boy woke from death! Just yesterday on the road He said to a leper, 'Be clean,' and as I looked, the leper's skin cleared and

"His power is greater than any man's!"

restored itself, and he was whole."

A slight gasp came from the shadow where Amrah sat. No one saw her scurry down the stairs and out into the street.

"We sit in the desert and wait," continued Ben-Hur. "The Galileans grow restless. Their swords are burning in their hands. Tomorrow Jesus the Nazarene, He who is said to be the coming King, will come to the temple here. Then we will know what sort of king He is."

"The Lord lives, and so do the words of the prophets," said Simonides. "Tomorrow will tell indeed."

Balthasar nodded, smiling.

That night Amrah hurried down the street and out of the city. She went down into the eastern valley. The dark green side of Mount Olivet was dotted with white tents. Many people had come to Jerusalem

Amrah scurried down the stairs.

for the Passover celebration, which was the next day.

She went past the garden of Gethsemane, past the tombs at the meeting of the Bethany roads, past the pool of Siloam, past the King's Garden, until she came to the Hill of Evil.

Many caves were cut into the hill. It was a forbidden place. Here lived—and died—the lepers. The Jewish law condemned lepers to live here. Anyone in Jerusalem who caught the disease must come to this hill to live out the rest of his or her miserable life. Food was brought near the hill daily from the city. The lepers would come down the hill, take what food they could, and return to their caves.

All through the night Amrah sat at the bottom of this hill. When the sun topped the eastern slopes she climbed up the path to the hill. She did not stop at the food-drop point

Amrah sat at the bottom of the hill.

but instead hurried on up the forbidden path until she came to a woman sitting in front of a cave.

The woman's face was uncovered. It was ghastly white and shriveled. On seeing Amrah, she threw her hood over her face. "Unclean! Unclean!" she cried. "Amrah! What are you doing? Have you lost your senses? You know the law. Oh, Amrah, now you cannot go back. You must remain here and die with us!"

Amrah knelt to the ground. She was so excited she could barely speak. "Your son Judah was at the house last night," she said. "He told us of the Man who is called Jesus of Nazareth. This Jesus has the power to heal. He made a leper clean!"

Ben-Hur's mother stood up. She was shaking. "How does my son know this?" she asked.

"He has followed the Nazarene and has

"How does my son know this?"

seen Him do these things," said Amrah. "The Nazarene is coming to Israel today! He can heal you and Tirzah. Come! You must come with me to the road. We will wait for Him there."

Now Tirzah came out of the cave. "Who is this Man Amrah speaks of, Mother?" she asked.

"If He does what Amrah says, He must be the Messiah," said her mother. "Many years ago the story went around that He was born in Bethlehem. I remember it well. That must have been thirty years ago; He would be a man by now. Could it be He?"

"It is said the Nazarene was born in Bethlehem," said Amrah. "Everyone is talking of Him. When your son spoke of Him last night, suddenly hope sprang up in my heart. You can be made well—I believe it! Come. We must hurry!"

"He can heal you and Tirzah. Come!"

Trembling, the mother turned to Tirzah. "Let us go," she said.

The three picked their way among the rocks covering the western slope of the hill, Tirzah and her mother moved very slowly. In the three years since their deliverance from the dungeon, the disease had eaten through their bodies, leaving them more dead than alive. Their limbs were like those of skeletons, their faces like those of hideous old hags.

When they reached the bottom of the hill, they slumped to the grass by the side of the road and waited there till morning.

It had been nearly three years ago that Amrah had heard the news of the release of the prisoners from the dungeons. The message had come to her one night that two women, lepers, had gone from the city to the lepers' colony. Amrah had gone

They moved slowly to the road.

there and found them, but Ben-Hur's mother pleaded with Amrah not to tell her son where they were. "If he knew we were lepers, he would come here and die with us," his mother said. So Amrah had kept their secret, coming to the hill daily to bring food for them. Every time Ben-Hur came to the house to visit, he asked of his mother and sister, and every time Amrah had to lie and say she had not heard anything, though her heart nearly broke.

Now as the three women waited by the road, Amrah's joy was nearly complete. First Ben-Hur had returned, and now, very soon, his mother and sister would be whole again.

The next day, people started coming down the road from the city. They came shouting and waving palm branches. More and more came shouting, "Hosanna! Hosanna to the King!"

"Hosanna! Hosanna to the King!"

And then the King came from the other direction, riding a donkey. A huge crowd came with Him, shouting and dancing.

"These two crowds will meet right here," said Tirzah. "The Master will never hear us call to Him in all this noise."

The crowds did meet right there. Thousands of people shouted praises to God while Ben-Hur's mother fell on her knees and clasped her hands.

The Nazarene seemed unaware of all the people and the clamor. He was looking at Tirzah and her mother. He rode up to them.

Suddenly people noticed the lepers. "The lepers!" they screamed. "Kill them! Stone them!" Several people began picking up stones to throw. The Nazarene simply held up His hand, and the people stopped as though struck.

"O Master!" cried Tirzah's mother. "You

"The lepers! Kill them!"

see our need. You can make us clean. Have mercy on us."

"Do you believe I am able to do this?" he asked.

"You are the One of whom the prophets spoke," she answered. "You are the Messiah!"

He smiled. In that smile was the look of a loving Father and a powerful King. "Your faith is great," he said. "It is done for you, just as you believe." He stared at them a moment longer, then turned back to the road.

Slowly crowds passed. Before the last had gone by, the miracle was complete. The women felt a tingling start deep in their bones, then spread throughout their bodies. As Amrah stood speechless, the two women were transformed before her eyes.

Now the crowds had passed. Only one man was still walking down the road. The

The two women were transformed!

three women were hugging and weeping and praising God. The man came closer.

"Mother!" cried the man. "And Tirzah!"

"Judah! My son!"

Ben-Hur had been following the crowd into the city. Farther behind, yet unseen, were two legions of his Galilean troops. And there before him stood his mother and sister. They were just as he remembered them, so long ago. His mother had a few strands of gray hair now, though her face seemed just as young. And Tirzah was a woman now, even more beautiful than he remembered.

Now mother, son, and daughter embraced and wept and laughed. And as Ben-Hur wept, all the years of bitterness, of pain, of hate, of desire for revenge, washed off of him like dirt in a gentle rain.

Two days later, the crowds had gathered

The three embraced, wept, and laughed.

again. Thousands and thousands of people seethed around a hill called Golgotha, but now no shouts of praise to God, no singing, no laughter.

The Nazarene hung from a tall wooden cross on the top of the hill. Two other crosses were there, from which hung two common criminals. From the masses of people came taunts and curses and screams of hatred.

A crown of thorns encircled the Nazarene's head. Blood covered Him, head to foot. An inscription above Him read, JESUS CHRIST, THE KING OF THE JEWS.

In the vast crowd stood Ben-Hur, his mother and sister, Balthasar, and Esther. Simonides sat propped up in a litter raised on supports.

What had happened? How had the crowds turned so suddenly, so viciously, against their King? The twelve disciples

Crucified!

had deserted Jesus; the Galilean troops had deserted Ben-Hur. The hatred of the Jews for this Nazarene was unimaginable. He had come to their cities and spoken of a new kingdom. He had said, "I am the bread of life. Anyone who comes to Me will never again be hungry. I am the resurrection and the life. No one comes to the Father but by Me."

He had healed the sick, cast out demons, made the blind to see, the lame to walk. He had raised the dead. Thousands and thousands from all over had called Him the King, the Messiah, the Son of God.

And now he hung dying on a cross.

Tears poured down Balthasar's face. Simonides stared vacantly. Esther shook with sobbing. She looked at Ben-Hur.

"Is it still too late?" she asked. "Can you not save Him?"

Ben-Hur's face was strangely peaceful.

"Can you not save Him?"

He shook his head sadly. "He has all the power of God at His command," he said. "He could save Himself if He wished. This is as He wills it."

Balthasar nodded. "O Lord!" he said. "To think I would live to see this horrible day! This is the day of damnation, the day of darkness." He closed his eyes and raised his tear-streaked face to heaven. "Yet I know that He will rise," he said. "On the third day He will rise, as it is written. And He will live, and will rule. And His kingdom will last forever and ever. It is written."

And now the tears came pouring down Simonides's face. "Ah, dear God in heaven!" he said. "I see at last. I believe. You are the Son of God!"

"Yes, Lord," said Ben-Hur, "Your kingdom is not of this world."

Suddenly the sky grew dark. The crowd grew deathly quiet.

Suddenly the sky grew dark.

The darkness hung over the land for three hours. Then Jesus cried out, "It is finished!" His head dropped to His chest. Then the ground began to tremble and the crowds began to run. They went stumbling over the rolling ground, screaming, weeping, tearing their hair, beating their breasts.

But Ben-Hur's group stood still, with raised arms, and praised God in tearful voices. Ben-Hur put his arm around Esther, and they worshipped God together.

He had found peace at last. He had found his mother and sister. He had found love, the beautiful Esther. And he had found his King. He could see the kingdom now—could feel it. It was rich and vast and growing, growing, growing. It was in his heart.

The kingdom was in his heart.

The kingdom was in his heart.

Special
Chronicles of Faith
Preview

The Pilgrim's Progress

"We are doomed!" he cried.

1

CHRISTIAN FALLS

The man stood in the field outside the City of Destruction and cried out in terror, "What shall I do?"

His clothes were ragged, and his back was bowed as if with a heavy load on his shoulders. He was reading a book, and what he read made him weep and tremble. His name was Christian.

That night at home, he tried to hide his anguish from his family but could not. He burst out, "We are doomed! I have learned that unless we escape this city, we will all be burned by fire from heaven."

His wife and sons were astonished. "You have taken a fever," said his wife. "Go to bed now. Sleep will settle your wits."

But Christian could not sleep. He tossed and he turned. In the morning he said, "I am worse yet. And this burden is even heavier."

And this went on for many days.

Christian's friends, even his family, scorned him. "He has gone out of his mind!" they said.

So he spent his days alone, walking in the fields, reading in his book, sometimes praying, sometimes weeping. One day as he stood reading he cried, "What shall I do to be saved?"

Just as he said this a man, tall and strong, walked up to him. "My name is Evangelist," said the man. "What troubles you so?"

"Oh, sir," said Christian, "I have read here that because of the bad things I have done, I will die and be punished forever."

Evangelist then handed Christian a roll of paper. On it was written, "Fly from the wrath to come."

"Which way?" cried Christian.

"Follow the light there," said Evangelist, pointing across a wide field. "You will come to a wicket gate. Knock at the gate, and you will be told what to do."

Christian saw the light shining far away,

"What shall I do to be saved?"

where the man pointed. Now he began running toward it. At last he felt some hope.

"Come back, fool!" came a cry from behind. Now two men from the city, whose names were Obstinate and Pliable, caught up with Christian and grabbed him by the arm.

"We saw you running away," they said. "We have come to bring you back."

"Never!" said Christian. "You live in the City of Destruction, which will be destroyed by fire. I go to find life."

And Christian told them of things promised in the book he had, of a life that lasts forever, a life free to all who flee the coming destruction.

"You have lost your wits, crazy fool!" said Obstinate, and he turned back.

But Pliable said, "If this life indeed be true, then I would seek it with you."

And so they set out together.

As they walked, Christian read to Pliable from the book. "There is a kingdom that will last

"We have come to bring you back."

forever, and we will live forever in that kingdom, wearing crowns of glory and clothes that shine like the sun."

The men grew eager for these things. And as their eagerness grew, they began to fear that something evil was following them and would catch them before they reached the kingdom. They began to run.

Suddenly they tumbled into a bog and began to sink. Pliable struggled desperately to the side and dragged himself out. "So! This is the life your good book promises," he snarled. "Well, not for me!" And he turned back to the city.

Christian sank deeper in the mire. The load on his back was dragging him under. Just as the bog closed over his head, he felt a strong hand grab his arm, and he was pulled out onto dry ground.

Christian stood dripping filthy mud and looked into the kind face of his rescuer.

"My name is Help," said the man. "This bog is called the Slough of Despond. It is the dumping

A strong hand pulled him out.

place of all the fears and doubts of people who are lost in sin. If you look hard, you will see steps through it that the King has placed here. But watch carefully!"

Christian did watch carefully then and crossed the bog safely. As he went on he met another man, Mr. Worldly Wiseman from the Town of Carnal.

"And where are you going, and why so bent over as if with a heavy load?" asked the man.

Christian told him of his journey and of the man, Evangelist, who sent him.

"Fah!" said Wiseman. "Evangelist! His is the hardest road to follow. Come, I will show you a way that is easy, and where many pleasures await you."

Mr. Wiseman pointed to a high hill, where lived Mr. Legality in the city of Morality. "His is the first house you come to. He will ease that burden off you."

Christian eagerly set out for this hill. But as he started to climb, his burden grew heavier and

"Watch your steps carefully!"

heavier. Then suddenly, flames shot out at him from the hill. He fell down in terror.

"Christian! Why have you come this way?" came a voice. There stood Evangelist, untouched by the flames as they lashed around him.

So Christian told him of Mr. Worldly Wiseman and Mr. Legality.

Evangelist said, "Listen to what the Lord says: 'Try to enter the narrow gate, because that way leads to life.' All other ways lead to death. Mr. Legality only leads you away from the one place where you can leave your burden, which is your sins. That place is the Cross."

Christian's journey doesn't stop here!
It's only beginning.
See how it ends in
Chronicles of Faith: The Pilgrim's Progress.

Available wherever books are sold.